SUSTAINABLE WORLD

WASTE

Rob Bowden

HODDER
Wayland

an imprint of Hodder Children's Books

SUSTAINABLE WORLD

Energy • Environments • Food and Farming
Transport • Urbanization • Waste

For more information on this series and other Hodder Wayland titles, go to www.hodderwayland.co.uk

Sustainable World: Waste

Text copyright © 2003 Rob Bowden
Series copyright © Hodder Wayland
First published in 2003 by Hodder Wayland,
an imprint of Hodder Children's Books.

Reprinted in 2004

Commissioning Editor: Victoria Brooker
Book Designer: Jane Hawkins
Consultant: Dr Marie Harder

Book Editor: Margot Richardson
Picture Research: Shelley Noronha, Glass Onion Pictures

Series concept by: Environment and Society International –
Educational Resourcing

easi-er

British Library Cataloguing in Publication Data
Bowden, Rob
    Waste - (The sustainable world)
    1. Waste - Environmental aspects - Juvenile literature
    I. Title
    338
ISBN 07502 39832

Printed in China

Hodder Children's Books
A division of Hodder Headline Limited
338 Euston Road, London NW1 3BH

Disclaimer
The website addresses (URLs) included in this book were valid at the time of going to press. However, because of the nature of the Internet, it is possible that some addresses may have changed, or sites may have changed or closed down since publication. While the authors and Publishers regret any inconvenience this may cause the readers, no responsibility for any such changes can be accepted by either the author or the Publisher.

Cover: Forklift stacking recycled paper.
Title page: Rubbish litters this city roadside in Nigeria, creating a public waste problem.
Contents page: Waste plastic is sorted for recycling in New Delhi, India.

Picture Acknowledgements
Corbis (David H Wells) 17, (Robert Landau) 39; EASI-Images (Rob Bowden) 7 (bottom), 16, 23 (left), 25, 45, (Roy Maconachie) 22, 23 (right), 28; Ecoscene (L A Raman) 3, (Vicki Coombs) 8, (Jim Winkley) 11, (John Wilkinson) 12, (Erik Schaffer) 15, (Alan Towse) 19, (John Farmar) 32, (Wayne Lawler) 33, (Bruce Harber) 36, (Erik Schaffer) 40, (Amanda Gazidis) 43; Getty Images (V. C. L.) cover; Impact (Peter Menzel) 30, (Piers Cavendish) 37; Peter Menzel 2003 20, 21; Popperfoto 9, (Reuters/Bobby Yip) 13, (Reuters/Henry Romero) 26, (Reuters/Toshiyuki Aizawa) 29; Still Pictures (Mark Edwards) title page, (Mark Edwards) 5, (Edgar Cleijne) 6, (Emmanuel Vialet) 7, (Hartmut Schwarzbach) 10, (Mark Edwards) 18, (Adrian Arbib) 24, (Julia Etchart) 44; Topham Picturepoint 14, (Polfoto) 27, (ANP/Bob van den Cruysem) 34, (Polfoto/Jens Dresling) 42; Hodder Wayland Picture Library 35, (Angela Hampton) 38, (Angela Hampton) 41; Wiggly Wigglers Ltd 31.

363·728
Bow

X

weblinks

You don't need a computer to use this book. But, for readers who do have access to the Internet, the book provides links to recommended websites which offer additional information and resources on the subject.

You will find weblinks boxes like this on some pages of the book.

weblinks

For more information on acid rain around the world, go to www.waylinks.co.uk/series/susworld/waste

waylinks.co.uk

To help you find the recommended websites easily and quickly, weblinks are provided on our own website, **waylinks.co.uk.** These take you straight to the relevant websites and save you typing in the Internet address yourself.

Internet safety

➚ Never give out personal details, which include: your name, address, school, telephone number, email address, password and mobile number.

➚ Do not respond to messages which make you feel uncomfortable – tell an adult.

➚ Do not arrange to meet in person someone you have met on the Internet.

➚ Never send your picture or anything else to an online friend without a parent's or teacher's permission.

➚ If you see anything that worries you, tell an adult.

A note to adults
Internet use by children should be supervised. We recommend that you install filtering software which blocks unsuitable material.

Website content

The weblinks for this book are checked and updated regularly. However, because of the nature of the Internet, the content of a website may change at any time, or a website may close down without notice. While the Publishers regret any inconvenience this may cause readers, they cannot be responsible for the content of any website other than their own.

HODDER
Wayland

Contents

Why sustainable waste?

WE ALL PRODUCE WASTE. WHETHER AT HOME, school, work or at leisure, all human activities create waste of one form or another. You may not give much thought to the wastes you produce in a day, but if you did you would probably be quite surprised by both the variety and amount.

WORLD OF WASTE

The problem is that you are only one of almost 6.5 billion people on Earth whose activities all produce wastes as well. That said, not everyone produces the same amount of waste or indeed the same types of waste. In general, people living in the more developed regions of the world such as North America and Europe generate more waste than those living in less developed regions such as Asia or Africa. The fact remains, however, that at the start of the twenty-first century the amount of waste generated is growing year by year.

The endless generation of waste means landfill sites such as this in the UK are quickly becoming full.

DATABANK

An average UK person throws away the equivalent of seven to ten times their own bodyweight in rubbish every year.

BREAKING POINT

As the volume of waste increases so does its impacts on people and the environment. Some of these impacts are very visible, such as litter on the streets of towns and cities, or lakes and rivers polluted by waste chemicals. Others are less visible, but extremely serious, such as the threat of climate change due to emissions of carbon dioxide (CO_2) and other greenhouse gases into the atmosphere. Around the world there are signs that something must be done to reduce the problems caused by waste and, more importantly, to reduce the amount of waste generated in the first instance. Failure to act could push the Earth's ability to support life beyond breaking point. This problem has been demonstrated by the environmental group, Friends of the Earth. They believe that if everyone were to generate waste at levels similar to people living in the UK or USA today, then the equivalent of eight planets would be needed to sustain such a wasteful world in the future.

Coal-fired power stations release large volumes of CO_2 and other waste gases into the atmosphere.

AN ALTERNATIVE FUTURE

Thankfully, there is an alternative future, one built around the idea of sustainable development. Sustainable development is about using and managing resources for the benefit of people today, whilst protecting and conserving them for the benefit of future generations. This book will explore the vital role waste has to play in a more sustainable world.

> ### OPINION
>
> The US is sinking under an endless avalanche of waste, with no credible plan of action in sight.
>
> *Lynn Landes,*
> *founder of Zero Waste America*

The waste problem

AT ONE TIME HUMAN ACTIONS PRODUCED wastes that could be absorbed by the environment. This was because they were mainly organic wastes (wastes that decompose naturally) produced from activities such as farming, hunting and fishing. The human population was also relatively small and in 1800, around the time of the industrial revolution, was still less than one billion people.

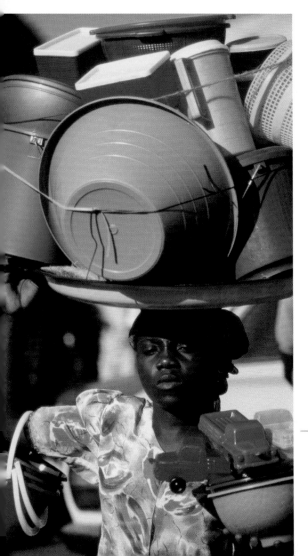

Plastic goods made from oil, such as these for sale in Ghana, present new waste challenges.

THE PRICE OF PROGRESS

From the time of the industrial revolution, a series of scientific and technological breakthroughs have allowed humans to manipulate the natural environment for their own benefit. These breakthroughs have brought us many things that we today take for granted, including new materials such as plastics and nylon, and products such as cars, televisions and white goods (washing machines, fridges, etc). Scientific advances also allowed for dramatic improvements in people's health and life expectancy. As a result, world population grew rapidly, reaching 2 billion by 1927 and then accelerating extremely fast to reach 4 billion in 1974 and 6 billion by 1999. The world population continues to grow by around 80 million people a year and is estimated to reach 9 billion by around 2050.

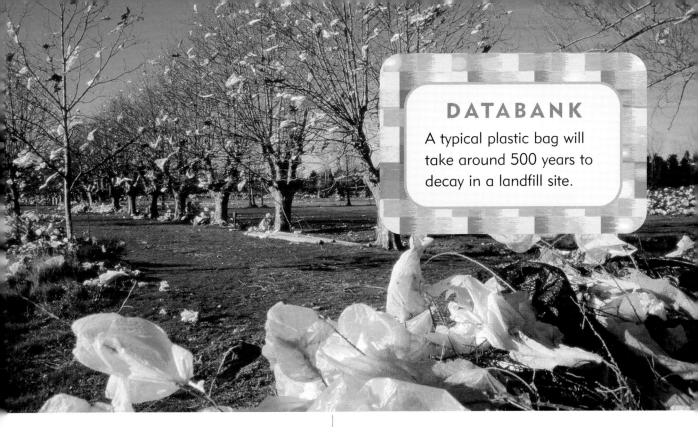

DATABANK

A typical plastic bag will take around 500 years to decay in a landfill site.

Discarded plastic bags in France caught among trees, having been blown there by the wind.

This progress comes with a price, however, often paid in the amount of waste that is produced. For example, the discovery of oil that led to the development of plastics and the spread of the motor car has also led to serious waste problems such as how to manage waste plastics and the polluting emissions of motor vehicles. Progress has also led to an energy hungry world, with most of this demand being met by fossil fuels. The problem is that when fossil fuels are burned (to release their energy) they emit carbon into the atmosphere which mixes with oxygen to become carbon dioxide – one of the major greenhouse gases responsible for climate change. Global carbon emissions increased from 1,637 million tonnes in 1950 to 6,399 million tonnes by 2000. This increase, of an incredible 390 per cent, is much greater than the 240 per cent increase in population over the same period. It shows that the amount of waste produced is increasing at a rate faster than population growth, meaning each of us is producing more waste than in the past.

Incineration of waste along this roadside in Kenya causes choking, hazardous fumes.

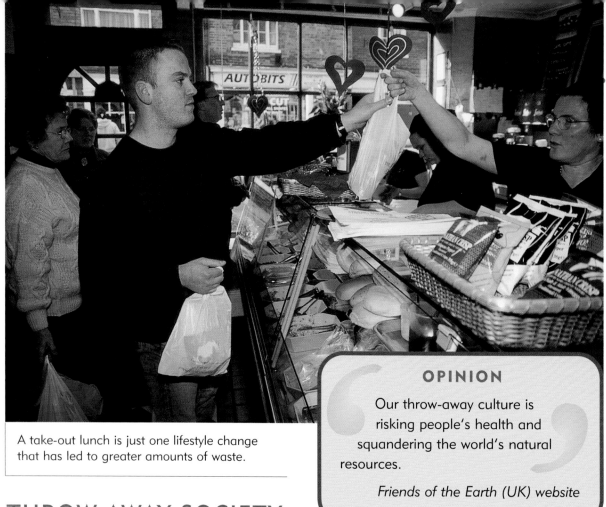

A take-out lunch is just one lifestyle change that has led to greater amounts of waste.

THROW-AWAY SOCIETY

Some of the main reasons we each produce more waste than in the past are due to changing lifestyles and increased wealth. Greater wealth means people have more money to spend and are more willing (and likely) to pay for convenience in the goods they buy. This has led to an enormous increase in waste because of the packaging involved in convenience foods.

Take, for example, a typical office worker buying his or her lunch from a sandwich shop. The chances are that the sandwich is packaged (more often than not in plastic), as is a packet of crisps and perhaps a chocolate bar or cake they have for dessert. They may also buy a coffee in a disposable polystyrene or paper cup, or perhaps water or a soft drink in a plastic bottle, carton or aluminium can. All of this will probably be packed in a plastic bag from the store itself and so, very quickly, this single office worker has created a significant amount of waste. Compare that to the office worker of twenty or thirty years ago who was more likely to have brought lunch from home in a re-usable lunch box and a bottle or flask. This would have produced only a minimal amount of waste, if any at all.

Convenience is only one factor that has led to greater waste, however. There is also enormous pressure from advertisers to constantly try new products as fashions change or to replace existing goods with new or updated ones. The mobile phone market is a good example of this. In the UK, for example, people replace their handsets, on average, every eighteen months, despite them having a useful life of around eight years. This wasteful practice results in some 15 million handsets being replaced each year, many of which are simply thrown away. The impact of this waste is significant. For example, the cadmium from a single mobile phone battery is sufficient to pollute around 600,000 litres of water (about a third of an Olympic swimming pool). Most mobile phones are simply dumped in landfill sites where such wastes can easily escape into the environment. The combination of convenience, and constantly changing fashions and technology, have created a consumer society that is also a throw-away society – and far from sustainable.

DATABANK

In the UK some 1.5 million computers are thrown away every year, most of them ending up in landfill sites.

Mobile phone companies constantly encourage people to upgrade their phones and the old ones are often just thrown away.

TYPES OF WASTE

Waste can be classified into many different types. For example, it can be described as solid, liquid or gaseous waste, or as organic and non-organic waste. One of the most common ways to classify waste (as used by many governments) is as municipal solid waste (MSW) and industrial waste. Waste can also be classified as hazardous.

MSW is the waste that you and I have most contact with. It includes the waste from our own homes and gardens and from the schools, offices, shops, restaurants and hospitals within our communities. It also includes the waste from public litter bins and local refuse collection centres ('tips' or 'dumps' as they are often known). When most people discuss waste it is this type of waste that they are normally talking about.

Industrial waste comes from industrial processes such as mining, energy production, manufacturing and agriculture. Industrial waste can be produced on an enormous scale. In mining, for example, vast quantities of material are removed from the ground in order to extract the desired mineral. It is not unusual for over 75 per cent of this to end up as waste,

Municipal Solid Waste (MSW) is collected from homes in Bielefeld, Germany. MSW is the waste we have most day to day contact with.

Only a fraction of the iron ore extracted from this Australian mine is mineral that can be used.

known as 'tailings'. Other industries, such as the paper industry, produce massive quantities of waste water, much of it contaminated with chemicals from the production process.

Hazardous waste presents a danger to human health and/or the environment. As well as specific sources of hazardous waste, such wastes can also be found in MSW and industrial wastes. For example, chemicals used in certain industrial processes or the heavy metals used in batteries can both be hazardous if not properly handled. Agricultural chemicals can also be hazardous, such as some pesticides which can lead to growth disorders, blindness or even death in both wildlife and humans. Among the most hazardous wastes are radioactive wastes. These are found in hospitals where they are used in x-ray departments, for example, and are produced in larger quantities by the nuclear energy industry. The most dangerous nuclear wastes can remain hazardous to life for an incredible half a million years!

WASTE DISPOSAL

Just as there are different types of wastes, there are also different methods of waste disposal. The main methods include burying mixed waste in landfill sites, burning it in incinerators, and re-using or recycling sorted waste. Of these, only the re-use or recycling of waste is truly sustainable. Unfortunately though, the vast majority of waste is presently disposed of in landfills or by incineration. In the USA, for example, around 57 per cent of MSW is disposed of in landfills, whilst in the UK this rises to 78 per cent and to over 90 per cent in Greece and Mexico! The incineration of MSW is a more popular disposal method in Japan, Denmark and Sweden where it accounts for 69, 54 and 42 per cent of MSW disposal respectively.

Incinerators reduce solid waste to ashes, but can release toxic pollutants into the atmosphere.

DATABANK

Composition of MSW in the USA (2000)

Paper	37.4%
Yard Trimmings	12.0%
Food Scraps	11.2%
Plastics	10.7%
Metals	7.8%
Rubber, Leather, and Textiles	6.7%
Glass	5.5%
Wood	5.5%
Other	3.2%

Source: US Environmental Protection Agency

Burying waste simply buries the problems associated with waste. Many wastes will take hundreds or even thousands of years to decompose, whilst others will release toxic substances (toxins) as they break down. In some landfill sites these toxins have been absorbed by rain water to form a substance known as 'leachate' that can then sometimes pass into the surrounding environment. In 1978, leachate that came from a landfill site in Love Canal, USA, contaminated local land and water and led to a school and housing estate being relocated.

Incineration of mixed wastes is not much better as the burning process can release toxins into the atmosphere, some of which are known to have links with cancer in humans, such as dioxins released from certain plastics and electrical components. Modern incinerators are able to reduce such emissions, but they still produce a toxic ash which must then be disposed of by other means.

THINKING AHEAD

Incinerating or burying waste does not solve the current waste problem, but by contaminating the surrounding environments simply shifts it for future generations to deal with. For waste to be managed more sustainably it is important that those creating wastes today think ahead and search for alternatives that do not pass on the problems to future generations. The responsibility lies with today's generations (people like you and me) to consider our lifestyles, limit the amount of wastes we generate, and dispose of those we do create in a safe and sustainable manner.

---
weblinks

To find out how a mixed waste incinerator works go to www.waylinks.co.uk/series/susworld/waste

---

A waste circuit board from the USA or Europe releases toxic fumes as it is burned in Guangdong province, China, to recover parts.

Towards sustainable waste

ENVIRONMENTALISTS HAVE BEEN CAMPAIGNING for more sustainable methods of waste management since the 1960s. It was at around this time that a number of high profile cases of waste disasters began to persuade people that the way waste was handled must change.

A woman holds a victim of Minamata disease, which provided early global warnings about the problems of uncontrolled wastes.

WARNING SIGNS

One of the earliest waste disasters began in 1953 when residents living in the Japanese fishing village of Minamata began to complain of illnesses such as headaches, convulsions and even blindness. By 1966, 43 people had died and 66 had become permanently disabled by their illnesses. By 1983, the death toll had passed 300 and as many as 6,000 claimed to be suffering illnesses and disabilities. This terrible human tragedy was caused by a nearby chemical factory discharging waste methyl mercury into the waters around Minamata. The poisonous mercury was absorbed into the food chain and poisoned the local inhabitants when they ate fish captured in the area.

At more of a global level, Scandinavia alerted the world to the problem of acid rain. This is caused by waste gases (mainly nitrogen oxides (NOx) and sulphur dioxide (SO_2) which are emitted when fossil fuels are burned). When these are released into the atmosphere they mix with water vapour to form an acidic solution that falls to the ground as rain, snow or fog. In the 1950s, people across Scandinavia began to notice that fish in many lakes were disappearing. This was due to the lakes becoming too acidic as a result of acid rain. In Sweden today, some 14,000 lakes suffer from the effects of acidification and the same is true for many lakes across other countries in Scandinavia, as well as the UK and parts of North America.

What makes acid rain a particularly interesting example is that it is 'long-distance' waste. The gases causing acid rain often affect areas far from their source as they are carried on the wind to distant locations. In Scandinavia, for example, it is estimated that 90 per cent of acid rain is caused by waste emissions blown mainly from the UK, Germany and Poland. The experience of acid rain in Scandinavia alerted the world to the fact that some wastes were a regional or even global problem and would require international co-operation to solve them.

— **weblinks** —

To find out more about acid rain
go to www.waylinks.co.uk/series/susworld/waste

DATABANK

A survey of European forests in 1999 revealed that one in four trees were damaged (suffering loss of leaves or needles). Acid rain was thought to be among the major causes.

These trees in the Harz mountains of Germany have been damaged by acid rain caused by waste gases in the atmosphere.

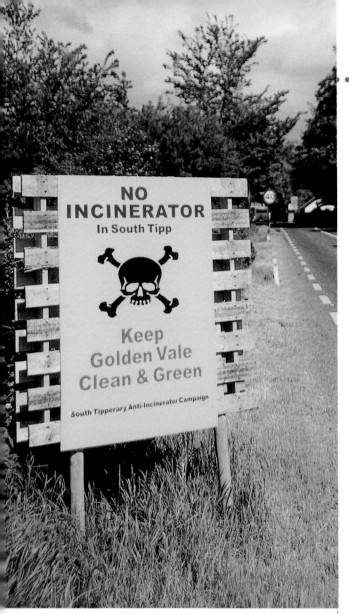

A roadside sign forms part of a local campaign to avoid a new incinerator being built in County Tipperary, Ireland.

CALL TO ACTION

Waste issues are today among the biggest concerns of environmental organizations around the world. Greenpeace, for example, has had a long-standing campaign against the nuclear energy industry and the wastes it generates.

Friends of the Earth, meanwhile, highlights waste as one of its priority campaigns with particular attention to the problems of landfill and incineration of mixed waste. More recently a number of organizations have been established that focus solely on the problems of waste. In the UK, for example, Waste Watch was established in 1987 to promote greater awareness of waste reduction, re-use and recycling – the so-called three Rs. A similar, Internet-based organization called Zero Waste America (ZWA) was established in 1996 in the USA.

As public awareness of waste issues has increased so too has their concern to do something about them. In particular, people have become concerned about the handling of waste in their own communities. Numerous local campaign groups have developed as a result. In fact, so widespread are such campaigns that there is probably one in your own community or a neighbouring one. A problem with many such campaigns is that their concern is with waste handling facilities close to where people live rather than with the problems associated with waste overall. Many of those involved in such campaigns would not have considered waste issues had they not been on their doorstep. This way of thinking has been given a special name: NIMBY, meaning Not In My Back Yard.

SPEAKING OUT LOUD!

Proposals for new waste incinerators or landfill sites often spark NIMBY campaigns in surrounding communities. Some of these have been extremely successful, such as the Guildford Anti-Incinerator Network (GAIN) in the UK. The actions of GAIN and its supporters helped to prevent the construction of a waste incinerator in their neighbourhood, but, more importantly, the attention given to waste issues has started a detailed debate on making the town of Guildford (near London) into a zero-waste community. The success of GAIN also inspired a local musician, Niamh Clune, to write a song called 'We Are The Voice' to encourage others to speak out on environmental issues. The song was performed at the opening ceremony of the World Summit on Sustainable Development in Johannesburg in August 2002.

weblinks

For more information about Waste Watch and its work go to
www.waylinks.co.uk/series/susworld/waste

OPINION

GAIN and its thousands of supporters will never give up the fight to prevent our children being exposed to the dangers of incinerator pollution and to develop alternative solutions.

Colin Matthews, Chairman of GAIN

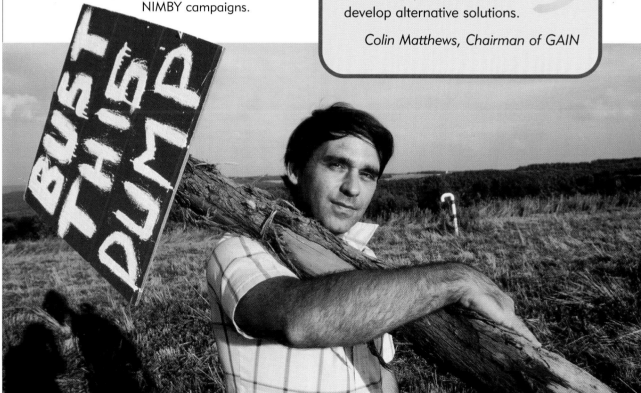

Resistance to waste handling facilities in local neighbourhoods such as here in New York state, USA, have become known as NIMBY campaigns.

LOOKING TO ALTERNATIVES

Whilst the public is often quick to oppose mixed waste handling facilities such as incinerators and landfills, the public response to alternatives is often less immediate. For example, many people know about the benefits of recycling, but fail to recycle everything that they could. Similarly, many people choose not to buy goods made with recycled materials as they believe they are of lower quality than goods made with raw materials. Such attitudes will have to change dramatically if waste is to be sustainably managed in the future.

Thankfully, progress has already been made in encouraging people to consider the alternatives to waste disposal. The most obvious example of this is recycling and today, in more developed countries at least, recycling bins are a common feature in many villages, towns and cities. These provide central collection points for people to sort and recycle some of the main items found in a typical household's waste such as glass, paper, cans and clothes.

Recycling of glass is practised by many people, but in reality is only a very minor part of the bigger waste problem.

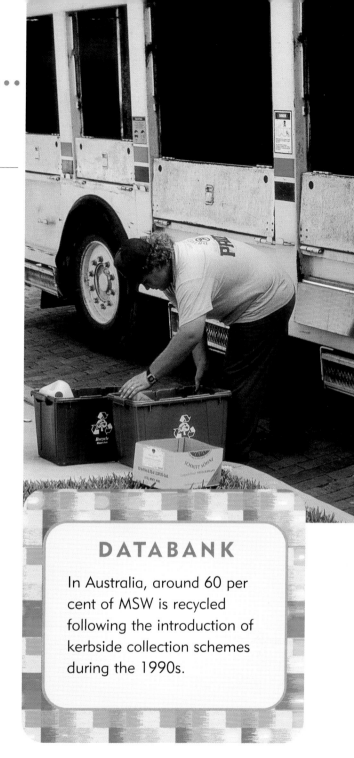

Kerbside collection schemes like this in Florida, USA, have helped to boost recycling rates.

Kerbside recycling schemes – where households sort waste into different materials for collection from outside their houses – have also become popular in some countries. In the USA, for example, the number of kerbside collection schemes grew from just 1,000 in 1988 to over 9,000 by 1998. The kerbside schemes have helped the USA achieve significant improvements in its recycling of MSW which increased from just 8 per cent in 1990 to around 32 per cent by 2001. Similar schemes have helped other countries, including Switzerland, Holland and Germany recycle over 50 per cent of their MSW.

A GOOD START?

Recycling is certainly a good start in the struggle to solve the waste problem, but it is only a start. Recycling rates often only apply to MSW, which in turn can be only a small proportion of the total waste generated within a country. In the USA, for example, the Environmental Protection Agency has estimated that MSW makes up only around 2 per cent of all US waste. The other problem with recycling is that although it has increased in most countries, so too has the amount of waste being generated in the first place.

DATABANK

In Australia, around 60 per cent of MSW is recycled following the introduction of kerbside collection schemes during the 1990s.

For example, in Norway between 1995 and 1998, the total amount of waste generated increased by three times more than the amount that was recycled over the same period.

A US family with their typical weekly food shop. The packaged goods create a large amount of waste, including a growing amount of plastics.

BEYOND RECYCLING

Perhaps the greatest challenge to creating a future in which waste is sustainably managed is to move people beyond the relatively easy task of recycling. A far greater impact can be had by reducing the amount of waste produced in the first place and making the remaining waste easier to manage. Some waste reduction measures are very simple, such as refusing plastic bags when offered them in a shop, or using public transport instead of private vehicles to reduce harmful emissions. Others are more complex, such as dealing with the excessive packaging that many products (especially supermarket foods) are sold in. To reduce wastes such as these, businesses and industries will have to become actively involved in trying to reduce the amount of waste their products create.

GROWING MOUNTAINS

Reducing the amount of waste produced is essential to stop the growing mountains of waste that today plague so many

Most of the waste generated by the week's food shopping for this Turkish family is biodegradable and so has relatively little environmental impact.

countries. The problem is most serious in the more developed countries where the amount of waste generated per person increased by around 22 per cent between 1980 and 2000, and is set to increase by a further 30 per cent by 2020. In some countries the problems due to not acting are already clear to see. In the USA, for example, New York's landfill sites are now full and so the city has started transporting its waste beyond the city limits. A convoy of lorries, that if put together would stretch for almost 14 km, carries away around 11,000 tonnes of waste every day to landfill sites up to 480 km away. In the UK too, numerous landfill sites will be full before 2010 if waste production continues at present levels.

FORCING CHANGE

Some of those most concerned about the waste problem suggest that after over thirty years of persuading people to reduce wastes it is time for governments to take more direct actions that will force changes. They argue that by taxing any wasteful and polluting activities governments are able to influence businesses, industries and individuals alike to change their attitudes to waste. Such direct actions are gaining in popularity and demonstrate a willingness to take the waste problem more seriously. Some of these will be considered later in this book.

Sustainable waste in practice

F EW PEOPLE WOULD DISAGREE with the need to reduce waste, but turning this into practice is more complicated because many people are used to a lifestyle that generates a great deal of waste. The challenge is to persuade people to adopt a lower-waste lifestyle, but some resist such changes in the belief that it would mean a lower quality of life. In fact, evidence suggests this is far from true and that a low-waste lifestyle normally improves quality of life as it creates a cleaner and healthier society and saves money for individuals and governments alike.

WASTE NOT WANT NOT

People in less developed countries produce, on the whole, far less waste than those living in more developed countries. This is partly because they are less wealthy and so their consumption levels are considerably lower. However it is also because they value resources more highly and often don't treat them as wastes at all. Across much of Africa, for example, containers such as the plastic drums

A water seller in Kano, Nigeria, re-uses plastic drums that once contained vegetable oil to transport water to his customers.

that food oil comes in are cleaned out and sold as strong and durable water containers. Old tyres are used to make tough rubber sandals, and the tyres' reinforcing wires are stripped out and used to make fishing baskets. Tin cans are re-used to make small oil lamps whilst bigger pieces of metal are beaten into shape to make small stoves. In fact almost anything that can be used again will be and this philosophy helps to keep waste levels relatively low. In creating a more sustainable future there is much that could be learned from people who have for many years, found creative ways of re-using resources instead of just dumping them as wastes.

Left: Oil lamps and metal stoves made from recycled waste in Uganda.
Right: Nigeria boys with go-carts made from scrap.

THE THREE Rs

The most frequently used model for a sustainable waste policy is that of the three Rs: a simple order of priority that says we should first try to Reduce the amount of waste produced, secondly look for ways to Re-use wastes, and thirdly Recycle as much waste as possible. Only then should any remaining products be disposed of as genuine waste, but even these can have uses as we shall see. Let us now look at each of the three Rs in more detail.

Buying unpackaged fruit and vegetables reduces household waste and is often cheaper too.

WASTE REDUCTION

The most efficient way to tackle waste is to reduce the amount produced in the first instance. Most industries, businesses and households could significantly reduce the wastes they produce with relatively minor changes in the way they operate. Where this has been done, substantial financial savings can also often be made. Households, for example, can purchase frequently used goods such as toilet rolls, cleaning products and basic foods (cereals, milk, pasta, etc.) in bulk. This reduces the amount of packaging waste and will often work out cheaper too. They can also look for products that have less packaging waste, such as fresh fruit and vegetables instead of packaged ones.

For businesses, reducing wastes not only benefits the environment but makes good business sense too. This is because waste disposal is an expensive process, especially when toxic or hazardous materials require special treatment. A good example of this is the US-based 3M corporation which makes a variety of goods from stationery supplies to health products. In 1975 it began a 3P programme – 'Pollution Prevention Pays' – across its factories that, by the early 1990s, had reduced pollutants by over 600,000 tonnes and saved around US$500 million. It has further reduced wastes in the 1990s and continues to set ambitious waste reduction targets into the future.

Industries are now beginning to co-operate on waste reduction too. In Germany, for example, water companies serving Munich, Leipzig and Osnabrück are now paying local farmers to practise organic farming. This is because organic farming does not use harmful chemicals, many of which escape into local water supplies as wastes. It is cheaper for the water companies to work with farmers to encourage waste reduction than it is to clean farm chemicals out of the water supply.

Xerox, a major world supplier of office machinery, introduced tough waste reduction policies in 1991 and extended these to its suppliers in 1998. These included reductions in packaging, the elimination of toxic wastes and the clear marking of recyclable plastics used in its products. By 2000 these policies had helped Xerox to achieve recycling rates of 80 per cent for its solid waste and to reduce air emissions by 89 per cent between 1991 and 2001.

These washable nappies are a sustainable alternative to disposable nappies which can take up to 500 years to decompose in a landfill site. In the UK, some 8 million disposable nappies are thrown away every day.

DATABANK

As a result of its waste reduction policies, Xerox Corporation was able to generate cost savings of approximately US$47 million in 1999.

Mexican waste sorters collect PET bottles and crush them into bales, ready for recycling.

bottles are melted down and re-used as the raw material for manufacturing popular 'fleece' clothing.

FOLLOWING NATURE

In nature, wastes are continually re-used or recycled within local and global ecosystems: the wastes from one part of the ecosystem becoming a resource for another. As concern about sustainability has increased, businesses and industries are now looking closely at how they can follow the good example set by natural systems. They are realising that it is better to think of waste as a resource and to find new or alternative uses for it rather than disposing of it. In the textile industry, for example, waste plastic (Polyethylene Terephthalate, or PET for short) drinks

SETTING AN EXAMPLE

The idea of copying nature is perhaps best represented by the Danish industrial town of Kalundborg. Beginning in the 1970s the town developed one of the best-known waste re-use systems in the world. At the centre of the system are the Asnæs coal-fired power station (the largest in Denmark) and the neighbouring Statoil oil refinery. Owing to a shortage of water in the region, Statoil agreed to supply its treated wastewater to Asnæs for use in its cooling process. In return, Asnæs supplies Statoil with waste steam for use in its refining process. The waste steam is also supplied to a nearby chemical company and to around 20,000 households in Kalundborg itself where it forms part of a district heating system.

The re-use does not stop there however. The waste gases from the Statoil refinery are used as a cleaner fuel for the Asnæs power station and by Gyproc whose nearby factory makes plasterboard for the building industry. Gyproc also purchases one of its raw materials (calcium sulphate or gypsum) from Asnæs who produces it as a waste from a process called desulphurization that removes sulphur from coal which is released during its burning. Other partners in the Kalundborg system include a local fish farm, some commercial greenhouses, a chemicals company and a pharmaceutical plant. It has been estimated that by 1995, around 3 million tonnes of waste were transferred for re-use every year. Kalundborg stands as a good example of how wastes need not be a problem, but can in fact benefit others through their re-use as a valuable economic resource.

---

weblinks

To find out more about the re-use of waste products at home go to
www.waylinks.co.uk/series/susworld/waste

The Asnæs power station and Statoil refinery are at the heart of Kalundborg's resource re-use network.

A store holder in Nigeria shows off his shoes: waste shoes imported from Europe that he then reconditions, ready to be sold and used again.

EXTENDED LIFE

Another form of re-use is to give products an extended life. For example, the office machinery company Xerox now takes back all of its old machines. They are taken apart for use as spares, or are repaired and cleaned for sale as re-manufactured machines. Xerox's new machines are designed to be re-used in this way and so reduce wastes and provide lower cost business machines for those who can't afford new ones. A similar scheme called 'Fonebak' was launched in the UK in September 2002 to re-use discarded mobile phones by reconditioning them and sending them for resale in less developed countries.

The life of a product can also be extended by repairing it instead of disposing of it. Many goods could be easily and cheaply repaired and continue to provide a useful service for many years. Many companies now offer extended warranties to encourage the repair of their goods. Repairing goods also provides valuable jobs and reduces the use of raw materials needed to make replacement goods. Offering used goods to charities is another way to ensure that goods have an extended life and also benefit less fortunate people in your own community or around the world.

NEW LIFE

If waste products or materials cannot be re-used then the next best thing is to look for ways to give them new life by recycling them. The ability to recycle depends on two main factors: the material in question and the market for recycled materials. Some materials such as glass, metals and paper are relatively easy to recycle and there is a reasonably good demand for them. Aluminium, for example, used in soft drink cans among other things, can be endlessly recycled and made into new aluminium products. Using recycled aluminium also saves on energy, using up to 95 per cent less than is needed to make the same product with raw materials. Glass, too, can be repeatedly recycled, though in most circumstances it must first be sorted into different colour types. Paper, one of the most commonly recycled products, can only be recycled about four times before it begins to break down and deteriorate in quality, but this still helps to safeguard forests for future use.

DATABANK

Enough aluminum is thrown away by Americans every three months to rebuild the entire United States commercial airline fleet.

This gold was reclaimed from mobile phones that were discarded in Japan. Silver and other precious metals are also collected for re-use.

This waste tyre mountain in California, USA, will be burned to provide energy, but more innovative and less polluting uses are now being developed.

INNOVATIONS IN RECYCLING

Materials such as plastics are much harder to recycle. This is partly because there are many different types and they cannot be mixed. Plastics are also often only part of a product, such as the casing for a computer or mobile phone, which means they need separating before they can be recycled. Thankfully, as the recycling industry grows it is creating innovative new methods and uses for the recycling of more difficult wastes. For example HDPE (High Density Polyethylene) plastics such as those used for shampoo and milk bottles can now be recycled into a strong and durable material known as plastic lumber. This is increasingly used for things such as picnic benches, decking, small foot/cycle bridges, fencing and signs.

Another waste product that has seen considerable progress in recycling is vehicle tyres. In Western Europe alone an estimated 200 million tyres are disposed of each year with close to 60 per cent of them ending up in landfill sites or being burnt to generate energy. By breaking down tyres and producing a substance called rubber crumb, however, it is possible to recycle them into a wide range of applications. For example, they are used to make shock-absorbent surfaces for playgrounds and sports facilities or for the rubber backing of carpets and floor tiles. And new uses are being found all the time, such as in the USA where rubber crumb is mixed with asphalt to make a tough and durable road surface. In 2001, around 10 million tyres a year were being used in this process.

BACK TO BASICS

Recycling is not just about new technologies, however. One of the most basic forms of recycling is composting, the natural breakdown of organic material such as fruit, vegetable and garden wastes into nutrient rich soil. In the UK, around 38 per cent of domestic waste is thought to be organic content suitable for composting and yet in 1999 less than 3 per cent of domestic waste was composted in municipal or community schemes.

This figure does not include households who compost their own waste in a compost bin or wormery, but there is still great scope to increase composting levels. Wormeries are a particularly good way to compost kitchen waste, such as vegetable peelings, as they take up little room, are very efficient and can even be used indoors by people who do not have a garden.

---
weblinks

For more information on recycling of plastic go to
www.waylinks.co.uk/series/susworld/waste

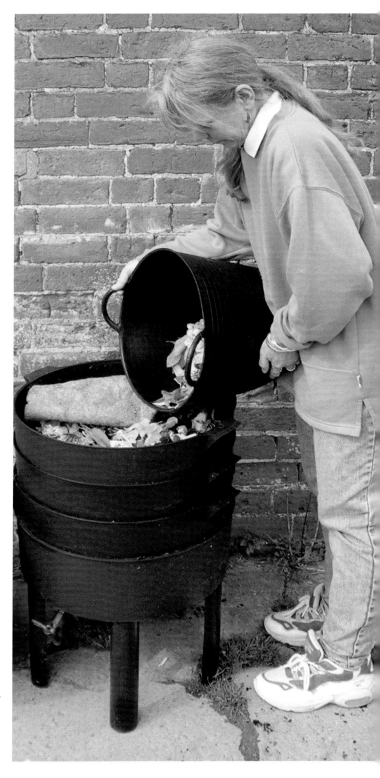

Kitchen waste tipped into the top of this wormery emerges as compost and liquid fertilizer at the bottom in as little as ten weeks!

Making sustainable waste work

• •

THERE IS GREAT SCOPE FOR IMPROVING recycling technology and methods in the future, but of equal, if not greater importance, is the challenge to change people's behaviour and attitudes to waste. If people begin demanding solutions to waste problems then it will encourage governments, industries and businesses to develop such solutions.

MIXED MESSAGES

Evidence suggests that people would like to manage their waste more sustainably. In England and Wales, for example, a survey by the Environment Agency found that nine out of ten people would recycle more if it were made easier. Despite this positive support, however, the UK has a

A local authority recycling centre in Weymouth, UK, collects many products that would otherwise be thrown away.

A coal-fired power station in Queensland, Australia. Australia has yet to agree to the Kyoto Protocol for reducing CO_2 emissions.

poor record on waste, with a recycling rate of only 11 per cent and a waste mountain that is set to grow by around one million tonnes a year! Other countries suffer similar contradictions between the attitudes and actions of their public. With such mixed messages on waste there is clearly a need for some form of intervention to encourage or even force more sustainable waste management.

TARGETING WASTE

One relatively simple form of intervention is the setting of waste targets. In the UK, for example, the government has set a target to recycle 25 per cent of household waste by 2005, putting pressure on all households, businesses and local authorities to do much better than at

present. As awareness of waste issues grows, most countries have now adopted waste targets of one form or another and some have even been adopted at a regional level. In the European Union (EU), for example, there are targets for the reduction and recycling of packaging waste and for the re-use and recycling of electrical wastes and even motor vehicles when they reach the end of their useful life.

At a broader level, international targets have been agreed to reduce some of the problems associated with waste. The Kyoto Protocol, for example, has set a target for reducing emissions of carbon dioxide to 5 per cent below their 1990 levels by 2008-12. Although several nations have yet to agree to the Kyoto Protocol (most notably the USA, Australia and Russia) it still marks an important international commitment to reducing wastes.

GETTING TOUGH!

Targets can be useful in highlighting areas where waste management needs to be improved, but as with many targets they are not always met and can be difficult to enforce. Some environmentalists believe

A man uses a swipe card to deposit waste in a community underground bin in Weert, The Netherlands.

that in order for real changes to be made, governments must get tough on waste and not rely on the voluntary actions of businesses and individuals. Where this has been done, substantial benefits have been seen. For example, in Switzerland fines of around 100 Swiss francs (£35) are imposed on households if they do not properly separate their waste for recycling and disposal. In Einzkries, Germany, household waste bins are fitted with an electronic system that measures the volume of waste disposed of and charges the residents accordingly. A similar scheme based on underground community bins in the Netherlands has been growing in popularity since it was started in 1997. Residents access the underground bins by swiping an electronic card to open them. The bin calculates the amount of waste that is deposited and coverts it into a charge to be paid by the household. In 1998 there were around 4,000 such bins in operation, but by September 2001 this had increased to 24,500 bins, reaching around 8 per cent of the Dutch population.

POLLUTER PAYS PRINCIPLE

The idea behind the policies used in the examples above is known as the polluter pays principle (PPP). This simply means that those who produce the most pollution (waste in this instance) should pay for it accordingly. It also means that individuals, businesses and industries that make efforts to reduce their waste output will end up paying less for waste disposal. PPP systems are therefore seen as encouraging greater uptake of the three Rs (see page 23). The benefits of policies based on PPP can be felt relatively quickly.

In Ireland, for example, a 0.15 Euro tax on plastic shopping bags introduced in March 2002, had, by the end of 2002, led to a tenfold reduction in the number of plastic bags used by Irish shoppers. On a broader scale the impact of applying the polluter pays principle to waste policy can clearly be seen in those countries where it has been tried. It is no coincidence, for example, that Switzerland, Germany and the Netherlands (the three examples given earlier) have some of the highest recycling rates in the world.

OPINION

The reduction [in plastic bags] has been immediate and the positive visual impact on the environment is plain to see. We are realising that by implementing practical measures such as this, the environment wins.

Martin Cullen, Irish Environment Minister

A customer in Ireland shows a strong re-usable bag use for grocery shopping. The use of such bags has increased following a tax on disposable bags introduced in 2002.

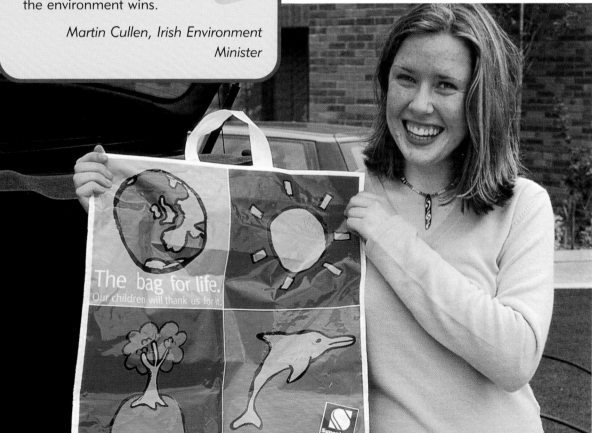

The bag for life.
Our children will thank us for it.

Customers in Denmark return their bottles to the supermarket for recycling. From 2002 they have been able to return drinks cans in a similar way.

environmental impact. Such decisions can prove unpopular, however, and Denmark has been in a long legal battle with the European Union which says the can ban is unfair on companies that produce their products in cans and wish to sell them in Denmark. In 2002 the Danish government was finally forced to abolish the can ban. Keen to continue its waste reduction policies, however, a refundable tax has been imposed on all cans to encourage people to return them for recycling. The government hopes that this 'deposit-and-return' system will lead to 95 per cent of drinks cans being returned to stores for recycling.

TAX SHIFTING

Some governments are concerned that introducing tough new policies on waste may prove unpopular with consumers (who are also the voters who keep them in power!). This is especially true if the policies involve charging people more for the wastes they produce. One way to overcome this problem is tax shifting. This is where governments raise taxes on environmentally damaging practices (such as waste generation) and in return lower taxes on incomes or products and services

BANNING WASTE!

Some governments have taken the decision to ban certain types of waste altogether by imposing laws on how products are sold. In Denmark, for example, the government imposed a ban on drinks cans in 1977 in favour of re-usable bottles that reduce the amount of waste generated and so have less

DATABANK

By 2002 Germany had shifted 2 per cent of its taxes on to environmentally destructive activities and as a result managed to reduce taxes on people's incomes by the same amount.

that benefit the environment. Tax shifting, like PPP, can have a rapid impact on consumer behaviour.

In the UK, for example, a lower tax on ultra low sulphur diesel (ULSD) than on normal diesel led to a rapid increase in ULSD sales, from 5 per cent of diesel sales in July 1998 to 43 per cent by February 1999. By 2000 the whole of the UK had converted to ULSD and so reduced sulphur emissions (one of the main waste gases responsible for acid rain) considerably. By applying tax shifting to energy use as a whole, several countries including Norway, Sweden, Germany, Italy and Finland have managed substantial reductions in their emissions of waste gases. For example, Finland introduced the first ever tax on CO_2 in 1990, and as a result had cut emissions by 7 per cent by 1998.

Cleaner diesel is now used by all diesel vehicles in the UK. A government tax on dirtier diesel helped to influence this change.

OPINION

It is increasingly clear...that countries are recognizing the power of tax systems...for shaping [the] economic decisions of individuals and businesses.

*Bernie Fischlowitz-Roberts,
Earth Policy Institute, USA*

This woman identifies the mark that tells her the envelopes she is thinking of buying are made with recycled paper.

KNOWLEDGE FOR ACTION

A major barrier to waste reduction is that people often lack the knowledge of how to go about it. There is a need to fill this information gap if sustainable waste management is to become a reality in the early twenty-first century. In truth, many opportunities and facilities for waste reduction exist on people's own doorsteps – they are just not aware of them. Governments, local authorities and those directly involved in waste management are now working to overcome such problems. In the UK, for example, a service for people to find recycling facilities using the Internet was launched in 2000 by a partnership of waste organizations, local authorities and over 700 businesses. Visitors to the 'recycle-more' website simply type in their postal code and the products they wish to recycle, and the service provides details of the nearest appropriate facility.

Most local authorities now provide information about waste reduction schemes and recycling facilities to residents living in their area. Many operate their own kerbside or communal schemes or have information about private schemes operating in their area. Many are also involved in direct education projects such as schools programmes to teach young people about the benefits of the three Rs. You may have experienced such a programme in your own school or community.

weblinks

To find out more about the UK's 'recycle-more' website go to www.waylinks.co.uk/series/susworld/waste

The office supplier, Staples, is one of many businesses that today use and offer an increasing number of recycled products.

CLOSING THE LOOP

One important area in which information needs to be improved is in raising awareness of where to buy products made from recycled materials. Recycling will only work properly when there is greater demand for the products made from recycled materials. This need is often referred to as closing the loop, so that people not only recycle, but purchase goods made from recyclable materials too. Numerous directories (many of them on the Internet) now exist to help consumers source and buy recycled produce. These are often aimed at households, but an increasing number are encouraging businesses and industries to buy recycled too. Some companies have adopted their own policies to promote recycled goods such as the office supply company Staples, one of the biggest in the world with over 1,400 stores in six countries. In 2002, around 1,000 of the 7,500 products that Staples stocked were recycled or contained recycled materials. The company also sponsors 'America Recycles Day', a day to raise awareness of recycling and recycled products.

weblinks

To find out more about America Recycles Day go to www.waylinks.co.uk/series/susworld/waste

Sustainable waste and you

C ONSUMERS LIKE YOU AND ME HAVE an important role to play in the future of waste management. We are able to send signals that will influence the actions of businesses, industries and governments alike to do something about waste issues. And of course we are able to take more direct actions ourselves too.

This German supermarket encourages recycling of excess packaging before shoppers even leave the store. Such schemes can help make recycling part of people's everyday routines.

CONSUMER POWER

Consumers are an extremely powerful force because their buying decisions can persuade manufacturers and retailers to change the ways in which they operate. After all, without contented customers, businesses would very quickly begin to lose money and may even go out of business. The trouble is that many consumers do not realize the power they have to influence change for the better and so businesses often continue wasteful practices such as the use of excessive packaging.

ACTIONS SPEAK LOUDLY

Our actions are of great importance and it is arguably here that consumers have the greatest power. For example,

Refusing disposable bags, and using your own re-usable bags instead, is a positive way to cut down on waste.

by purchasing goods that have less packaging, consumers send clear signals to manufacturers and retailers that they do not want the waste associated with heavily packaged goods. In the UK, a survey conducted in 2002 indicated that almost 90 per cent of consumers thought it was important that the supermarket where they regularly shopped was concerned about its effect on the environment.

With such high expectations, many supermarkets have begun to adopt various policies that promote the three Rs. Most now have re-usable 'bag for life'

schemes, for example, whereby customers buy stronger plastic bags and re-use them until they break. The supermarket will then replace the bag free of charge when it is returned to the store for recycling.

Recycling facilities are also a common sight at most supermarkets today and many offer in-store recycling facilities for their disposable plastic bags. One British chain, the Co-op, is particularly keen to promote the three Rs. In addition to promoting the use of recycled product packaging where possible, in 2002 it introduced the UK's first degradable plastic bag which takes just three years to degrade and leaves no toxins in the environment. This compares with over a hundred years before a normal disposable shopping bag even begins to break down.

LOCAL ACTION
Doing your bit

There are many ways that you can reduce wastes, but here are a few ideas to help get you started.

- Look for products that have less packaging, such as loose fruits and vegetables.

- Where possible, support re-use and refill schemes such as local milk delivery services.

- Buy in bulk products your family regularly uses to reduce packaging waste.

- Think before you buy! Do you really need it or could you rent or borrow an item instead?

- Have goods repaired rather than throwing them away and buy better made and more durable goods that have a longer lifespan.

- Ask retailers about their waste policies and whether their products are recyclable.

- Find out about recycled goods and buy them where possible.

- Join your local kerbside recycling service or take recycled waste to your nearest recycling centre.

- Set up a garden compost bin or a wormery to recycle organic kitchen waste.

A display in central Copenhagen, Denmark, is used to demonstrate how much litter is left in public places every day.

WORDS COUNT

On top of our actions, words are also very important. For example, when you go shopping you can refuse to accept a carrier bag for your goods and instead bring your own, or consider whether you even need one for smaller items that may fit in your pocket instead. Words can also be important in influencing waste policies in your own community. If you are concerned about the levels of waste or the lack of recycling facilities, for example, write to your local authority to find out what is being done about the situation, or even make some suggestions yourself.

You could have a similar influence in your school by suggesting that they conduct a survey of their waste patterns and look for ways to improve on them. The school could even earn money from recycling or setting up its own community recycling scheme. In the UK county of Suffolk, for example, Elmsett School, with just sixty pupils, has established a very successful school recycling centre. The centre serves the local community and is supported by the local authority and nearby businesses. Money raised from the sale of the recycled goods has been used to purchase new school equipment, to fund a part-time teacher and is now being saved to help fund a new school building.

---
weblinks

To find out more about Elmsett School Recycling Project go to www.waylinks.co.uk/series/susworld/waste

---

A stall at a 'Green Gathering' in Wiltshire, UK, sells clothing made from recycled fabrics that would otherwise be treated as waste.

Sustainable waste and the future

W E HAVE SEEN IN THIS BOOK that waste is a major challenge for this century and one that cannot be ignored. The world is already overflowing with waste, and much of it will still be around in hundreds or even thousands of years. This is far from sustainable and is polluting the land, water and air that all human and animal life depends on for their survival.

A GROWING PROBLEM

The problem with waste is that it is being generated at a rate faster than solutions to waste problems are being found. Some countries such as Hong Kong, the Netherlands and parts of the USA and UK, are literally running out of room to dispose of waste. There is no doubt that recycling has increased dramatically over the last thirty years and continues to do so, but if more waste is being produced at the same time, then the impact is only minimal. The key to a sustainable future is to reduce the amount of waste being produced in the first place and this will demand major changes in consumption

Litter on a beach along Venezuela's Caribbean coast is a reminder of the worldwide waste problem.

A market stall in Greenwich, London, sells toys, ornaments and even handbags, all made from colourful recycled tins and soft-drink cans.

OPINION

'Whilst we can't eliminate rubbish altogether, there are hundreds of ways in which we can cut down on what we throw away. So, whether we're recycling, finding new uses for 'junk' or simply reducing what we create in the first place, with a little effort, we can all make our homes cleaner and greener!

Rethink Rubbish website

patterns and attitudes to waste. Countries such as Switzerland, the Netherlands and Germany have demonstrated that such changes can take place, and over a relatively short time too. The key to their success has a great deal to do with the commitment shown by their governments, but it also relies on the co-operation of citizens like you and me.

SUSTAINABLE SOLUTIONS

Business and industries are slowly finding sustainable solutions to the problems of waste, such as the development of plastic lumber, degradable plastic bags and road surfaces made from old tyres. Financial incentives such as taxes and grants can be used to accelerate this process and are now being used in many countries as they struggle to meet national or international targets for waste reduction such as the Kyoto Protocol. The public too is involved in finding new uses for wastes including some creative solutions where wastes are being turned into toys or even art works. Perhaps the biggest change and the best solution to the waste problem is to stop thinking of goods as wastes. Instead we should think of them as resources that are simply waiting to be re-used in one way or another. In this way, waste can make a valuable contribution to a more sustainable world.

Glossary

Acid rain Produced when pollutants such as sulphur dioxide and nitrogen oxides (emitted when fuels are burned) mix with water vapour in the air to form an acidic solution. It is damaging to plants, trees, lakes and buildings.

Campaign A planned, organized action which aims to raise people's awareness of an issue.

Climate change The process of long-term changes to the world's climate (warming or cooling, etc.). Occurs naturally, but is today more as a result of human activities polluting the atmosphere.

Community A group of people who either live in the same area (e.g. village, town or district), share common interests and beliefs (e.g. the importance of recycling waste) or share both these characteristics.

Compost A mixture of organic household waste (e.g. vegetable waste and brown cardboard) and plants that have decomposed over time.

Consumers People who buy or use a resource, product or service.

Consumption The use of resources, products and services by consumers.

Ecosystem The contents of an environment, including all the plants and animals that live there. This could be a garden pond, a forest or the whole of planet Earth.

Emissions Polluting waste products (gas and solids) released into the environment. These include car exhaust and aeroplane fumes into the air and waste water and sewage into streams or the sea.

Food chain A series of organisms (plants and animals) each dependent on the next as a source of food.

Fossil fuels Fuels from the fossilized remains of plants and animals formed over millions of years. They include coal, oil and natural gas. Once used they are gone: non-renewable.

Greenhouse gas An atmospheric gas that traps some of the heat radiating from the Earth's surface. Human activity has increased the level of greenhouses gases, such as carbon dioxide and methane, in the atmosphere.

Hazardous Something that is dangerous to human health and/or the environment.

High Density Polyethylene (HDPE) A type of plastic used to make items such as bottles for shampoo, cosmetics and milk.

Incinerator A furnace where waste is burnt at high temperatures.

Industrial Revolution The period in the late eighteenth century and early nineteenth century (150-250 years ago) when new machinery and the use of fossil fuels to generate energy led to the start of modern industry and dramatic changes in the way people lived.

Kyoto Protocol Arising from a meeting held in Kyoto, Japan, in 1997. One hundred and sixty countries committed to reducing emissions of the six main greenhouse gases by 5.2 per cent by the year 2012.

Landfill sites Holes or hollows in the ground used for burying waste. Once full they are covered over and the land is often used for building or leisure activities.

Leachate A liquid formed as rainwater passes through a landfill site and carries diluted chemicals and metals with it.

Municipal Solid Waste (MSW) The solid waste produced by homes, schools, offices and shops.

Organic A product of living organisms that occurs naturally in the environment. Organic substances can be broken down by nature.

Packaging The container or wrapping that surrounds bought goods.

Polyethylene Terephthalate (PET) A type of plastic used to make soft drink bottles.

Radioactive substances Substances such as uranium or plutonium that emit energy in streams of radioactive particles. These particles are extremely harmful to humans and animals if they come into direct contact with them.

Recycling The collection and processing of used materials (e.g. glass, paper, cardboard and aluminium) so that they can be used again.

Resources The materials and energy used in making products or providing services.

Re-use To use something again, for the same or different purpose, instead of throwing it away.

Tailings The waste material from mining once the useful mineral has been extracted.

Toxin A poisonous substance which causes harm to human health and/or the environment.

White goods Domestic appliances such as washing machines, fridges and freezers that are today found in most homes in developed countries.

Wormery A sealed container in which worms are kept to break down organic kitchen waste.

Zero waste The recycling of all materials back into nature or the marketplace in a manner that protects human health and the environment.

Books to Read

21st Century Debates: Waste, Recycling and Re-use by Rob Bowden (Hodder Wayland, 2003)

Earth Watch: Waste Disposal by Sally Morgan (Franklin Watts, 2002)

Action for the Environment: Rubbish Disposal by Deborah Bedford (Franklin Watts, 2004)

Fun with Recycling by Marion Elliot (Southwater, 2001)

Useful Addresses

ENCAMS (Keep Britain Tidy Campaign)
Elizabeth House, The Pier
Wigan WN3 4EX
Tel: 01942 612639   www.encams.org.uk

Friends of the Earth
26-28 Underwood Street
London N1 7JQ
Tel: 020 7490 1555   www.foe.org.uk

Greenpeace
Canonbury Villas, London N1 2PN
Tel: 020 7865 8100
www.greenpeace.org.uk

Waste Watch
96 Tooley Street
London SE1 2TH
Tel: 020 7089 2100
www.wastewatch.org.uk

Wiggly Wigglers (Wormery supplier)
Lower Blakemere Farm, Blakemere
Herefordshire HR2 9PX
Tel: 01981 500391
www.wigglywigglers.co.uk

Zero Waste America
c/o Lynn Landes, 217 S. Jessup Street
Philadelphia, PA 19107   USA
(215) 629-3553
www.zerowasteamerica.org/

Index